Latimer Study 79

POSITIVE COMPLEMENTARIANISM

THE KEY BIBLICAL TEXTS

Ben Cooper

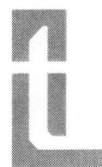

The Latimer Trust

Positive Complementarianism: The key Biblical texts © Ben Cooper March 2014.

ISBN 978-1-906327-21-7

Cover photo: Ballroom Dancers Blue 12© Alysta- fotolia.com

Scripture quotations marked (ESV) are from The Holy Bible, English Standard Version® (ESV®), copyright © 2001 by Crossway, a publishing ministry of Good News Publishers. Used by permission. All rights reserved.

Scripture quotations marked (NRSV) are from the New Revised Standard Version Bible: Anglicized Edition, copyright 1989, 1995, Division of Christian Education of the National Council of the Churches of Christ in the United States of America. Used by permission. All rights reserved.

Published by the Latimer Trust March 2014

The Latimer Trust (formerly Latimer House, Oxford) is a conservative Evangelical research organisation within the Church of England, whose main aim is to promote the history and theology of Anglicanism as understood by those in the Reformed tradition. Interested readers are welcome to consult its website for further details of its many activities.

The Latimer Trust
London N14 4PS UK
Registered Charity: 1084337
Company Number: 4104465
Web: www.latimertrust.org
E-mail: administrator@latimertrust.org

Views expressed in works published by The Latimer Trust are those of the authors and do not necessarily represent the official position of The Latimer Trust.

CONTENTS

1. **Introduction** 1
   - 1.1. *Positive complementarianism* 2
   - 1.2. *Anglican complementarianism* 3
   - 1.3. *'Complementarian' and 'egalitarian' defined* 3
   - 1.4. *Other, intermediate views* 6
   - 1.5. *The argument* 6

2. **The Creation in Genesis 1-3** 8
   - 2.1. *Genesis 1:1-2:3* 9
   - 2.2. *Genesis 2:4-25* 10
   - 2.3. *Genesis 3* 13
   - 2.4. *The wider literary function of Genesis 1-3 in Genesis as a whole* 14
   - 2.5. *Conclusions from Genesis 1-3 in its literary context* ... 15

3. **The New Testament Teaching** 17
   - 3.1. *Galatians 3:28* 17
   - 3.2. *Women in the Gospels and Acts* 18
   - 3.3. *Romans 16* 18
   - 3.4. *1 Corinthians 11:2-16* 19
   - 3.5. *Ephesians 5:8-6:9* 21
   - 3.6. *1 Peter 3:1-7* 22
   - 3.7. *Leadership in the Synoptic Gospels – Matt 20:20-28 et par.* 24
   - 3.8. *1 Corinthians 12:12-31* 26
   - 3.9. *Acts and Romans 16 revisited* 26
   - 3.10. *1 Corinthians 14:34-35* 28

4. **New Testament: 1 Timothy and Titus** 30
   - 4.1. *1 Timothy 2:8-15 – an important but complex negative case for gender complementarity in church leadership roles* 32
   - 4.2. *1 Timothy 3 and Titus 1 – a simple but neglected positive case for gender complementarity in church leadership roles* .. 39
   - 4.3. *Putting it all together* 40

5. **Further Conclusions** 41

1. Introduction

Roughly speaking, Christians calling themselves 'complementarian' believe on the basis of biblical evidence that the exercise of teaching and leadership roles within local churches should depend at least in part on gender. This is now very much a minority view across all the major UK denominations. It's a view that seems even more stubborn and eccentric against the wider cultural background. When on the 20 November 2012 the measure entitled 'Bishops and Priests (Consecration and Ordination of Women)' failed to gain a sufficient majority in the house of Laity of the General Synod of the Church of England, there was widespread incredulity from both media observers and politicians. At Prime Minister's Questions on the day after the result, David Cameron told MPs: 'I am very clear that the time is right for women bishops; it was right many years ago. The church needs to get on with it and get with the program'.[1] Rowan Williams (who was Archbishop of Canterbury at the time) commented, 'We have – to put it very bluntly – a lot of explaining to do. Whatever the motivations for voting yesterday [...] the fact remains that a great deal of this discussion is not intelligible to our wider society. Worse than that, it seems as if we are wilfully blind to some of the trends and priorities of that wider society'.[2]

Roughly speaking, Christians calling themselves 'egalitarian' believe that the exercise of teaching and leadership roles within churches should not depend *at all* on gender. Not surprisingly, many of them were dismayed by the 20 November Synod result. However, not all of them are entirely happy with the cultural and political pressure currently being placed on the Church of England. Writing soon after the Synod result in *The Times*, Tom Wright voiced his concerns.[3] 'Exhorting the CoE to "get with the program" dilutes the argument for women bishops,' he says:

> To argue that opposing women bishops would be 'putting the clock back,' or 'on the wrong side of history,' or absurd 'in this day and age,' is woefully inadequate. And until proponents of women bishops stop using such arguments, the *biblical*

---

[1] As reported in *The Telegraph*, 21 November 2012.
[2] Reported in *The Guardian*, 21 November 2012.
[3] *The Times*, 23 November 2012.

arguments for women's ordination will never appear in full strength. 'The Church that forgets to say "we must obey God rather than human authorities" has forgotten what it means to be the Church.'

Tom Wright then went on to argue that the real argument must be made from the Bible: to suggest that people who 'believe in the Bible' or who 'take it literally' will oppose women's ordination is 'rubbish'. Read properly, he argues, the Bible is fully supportive of the egalitarian view.

All of this means that those holding to a complementarian stance in the Church of England are in a very vulnerable position. They are vulnerable because they are adhering to a position that is profoundly and deeply counter-cultural. But if evangelicals such as Tom Wright are correct, then they are also vulnerable at a much deeper level: defending a position that is unbiblical and therefore, on their own terms, untrue and likely to bring the gospel into disrepute.

The aim of this short study is to make the claim that the complementarian view *is* biblical, over and against the dominant egalitarian consensus in the Church of England. Or, at least, the aim is to make a *sufficiently* strong complementarian case from the key biblical texts on gender roles – sufficient not to be ignored as the Church of England debates what to do with the minority who hold to it.

1.1. *Positive complementarianism*

This is to be a case for *positive* complementarianism. Given their minority and vulnerable position in the current debate, it is easy for complementarians to come across as negative and defensive. We are not helped in this by the fact that some of the key biblical texts (from 1 Corinthians 14 and 1 Timothy 2) are expressed in negative terms: what a women is 'not permitted' to do. The claim here, however, is that the complementarity between male and female portrayed as ideal in the Bible is a thoroughly beautiful arrangement: something to be admired and to aspire to. What's more, the complementarity functions to promote the gospel: to display it, and to act as a platform from which it can be proclaimed. It is part of the good conduct of God's household, 'the pillar and bulwark of the truth' (1 Timothy 3:15 NRSV).

1.2. Anglican complementarianism

This is also a case for an Anglican complementarianism, properly understood in relation to the 39 Articles of the Church of England. As a minority view in the Church of England at the moment it of course *seems* very un-Anglican. (Although, were one to consider the Anglican Communion as a global whole, things would look rather different.) Although the Articles are no longer considered by many to be relevant or applicable, they do summarize Anglican beliefs as they once stood, and for some, as they still stand. It also remains true that all Anglican clergy have to assent to them, along with the Prayer Book.

Article 20 states this:

Of the Authority of the Church.

The Church hath power to decree Rites or Ceremonies, and authority in Controversies of Faith: And yet it is not lawful for the Church to ordain any thing that is contrary to God's Word written, neither may it so expound one place of Scripture, that it be repugnant to another. Wherefore, although the Church be a witness and a keeper of holy Writ, yet, as it ought not to decree any thing against the same, so besides the same ought it not to enforce any thing to be believed for necessity of Salvation.

I shall be arguing in this study that the complementarian view, not the egalitarian view, is consistent with 'God's Word written'. I shall also be trying to avoid the error of expounding 'one place of Scripture, that it be repugnant to another'. Egalitarians tend to focus on texts such as Romans 16 and Galatians 3:28. Some complementarians tend to have an overly-exclusive focus on 1 Timothy 2:12. In what follows, we shall be attempting to do proper justice to *all* the relevant biblical texts.

1.3. 'Complementarian' and 'egalitarian' defined

I have said that Christians calling themselves 'complementarian' believe on the basis of biblical evidence that the exercise of teaching and leadership roles within churches should depend at least in part on gender, while those who might call themselves 'egalitarian' deny any such relation between role and gender. But it may be worth spending just a little more space on definitions before we begin.

Of the two, 'egalitarianism' is perhaps the easier to pin down precisely. The group *Christians for Biblical Equality* defines egalitarianism like this:

> CBE affirms and promotes the biblical truth that all believers – without regard to gender, ethnicity or class – must exercise their God-given gifts with equal authority and equal responsibility in church, home and world.[4]

There are several things to note in this definition. There is a claim to biblical authenticity. There is the linking of this issue with other issues of equality – ethnicity and class. There is a suggestion, at least, that believers have some kind of *right* to exercise their God-given gifts. And there is an application of the principle to every sphere of life: church, home and world.

Similarly, Rachel Held Evans defines the term like this:

> Christians who identify as egalitarian usually believe that Christian women enjoy equal status and responsibility with men in the home, church, and society, and that teaching and leading God's people should be based on giftedness rather than gender.[5]

Every role within a church structure open to men should therefore be equally open to women. In the Church of England, the current focus is of course on the role of bishop being as equally open to women as it is to men, on the same terms.

The term 'complementarianism' was coined as recently as the 1980s, in some of the early meetings of the Council for Biblical Manhood and Womanhood, as explained on their website:

> CBMW has been in operation since 1987, when a meeting in Dallas, Texas, brought together a number of evangelical leaders and scholars, including John Piper, Wayne Grudem, Wayne House, Dorothy Patterson, James Borland, Susan Foh, and Ken Sarles. These figures were concerned by the spread of unbiblical teaching. Under Piper's leadership, the group drafted a statement outlining what would become the definitive

---

[4] 'Mission Statement' downloaded from http://www.cbeinternational.org/?q=content/our-mission-and-history, 10 May 2013, 14:37.
[5] Downloaded from http://rachelheldevans.com/blog/mutuality-definition-terms, 10 May 2013, 14:42.

theological articulation of 'complementarianism,' the biblically derived view that men and women are complementary, possessing equal dignity and worth as the image of God, and called to different roles that each glorify him.[6]

However, there is a spectrum of views on how these differing roles should work out in practice in family, church and society. One end of the spectrum can be seen in the view of marriage seen in the Southern Baptist Convention's Baptist Faith and Message (2000), which says this about the wife's role in the household:

> She, being in the image of God as is her husband and thus equal to him, has the God-given responsibility to respect her husband and to serve as his helper in managing the household and nurturing the next generation.[7]

Contrast this with Mary Kassian, in a piece entitled 'Complementarianism for Dummies', in which she goes out of her way to distance complementarianism from merely culturally conservative views on the role and place of women.[8] Complementarianism is to be distinguished from 'traditionalism' (which she identifies with June Cleaver, the principal character in an American sitcom entitled *Leave It to Beaver*, who in the United States is frequently invoked as the archetypal suburban housewife of the 1950s). Complementarianism is to be distinguished from 'hierarchism' (comparable to the proletariat-bourgeois-type hierarchy that might exist in a class system). Complementarianism is to be distinguished from 'patriarchalism' (that is, the patriarchal, societal oppression of women). Rather, 'Complementarians believe God designs male and female to reflect complementary truths about Jesus'.

Mary Kassian's definition is worth noting, because some complementarians have used words like 'tradition', 'hierarchy' and even 'patriarchy' in describing their position. The danger with these terms is their potential association with social conventions that have very little to do with the radical impact of the gospel. We would expect the gospel to

---

[6] Downloaded from http://cbmw.org/history/, 10 May 2013, 14:58. A more complete definition can be found in the 'Danvers Statement on Biblical Manhood and Womanhood', http://cbmw.org/core-beliefs/.
[7] From http://www.sbc.net/bfm/bfm2000.asp, accessed 19 September 2013, 15:25.
[8] From http://www.girlsgonewise.com/complementarianism-for-dummies/, accessed 10 May 2013, 15:05.

have a behavioural impact whatever one's initial relational situation. It seems unlikely, therefore, that complementarianism, if true, is simply concerned with defending a certain cultural status quo. We shall be returning to this point several times in what follows.

1.4. Other, intermediate views

It is also worth noting before we begin that not all commentators on this issue would be happy to describe themselves as either 'egalitarian' or 'complementarian'. There is also a spectrum of intermediate views (as well as the spectrum of views within each position). For example, Michael Bird's recent study argues for something like complementarianism within marriages, but does not extend this to church or society.[9] As we shall see below, he argues that 1 Timothy 2 is concerned with a specific instance of false teaching in Ephesus, and that Paul is not making a general prohibition. Similarly, James Dunn, writing in the Church Times argues that the New Testament texts are *all* (including 1 Timothy 2) about husbands and wives and never about men and women in general.[10] So, again, any difference in role does not extend to church or society. John Dickson's recent contribution is slightly different, dealing with the specific question of whether women should give sermons in main church meetings.[11] He argues that whatever Paul is prohibiting in 1 Timothy 2, this shouldn't be applied today to women preaching.

1.5. The argument

Given these understandings of the terms 'egalitarian' and 'complementarian', the basic argument in what follows will be this:

> The creation accounts in Genesis 1-3 do indeed imply some sort of gender complementarity as an ideal for relations between men and women. The New Testament writers then explicitly

---

[9] Michael Bird's study has the unfortunate title *Bourgeois Babes, Bossy Wives, and Bobby Haircuts: A Case for Gender Equality in Ministry* (Fresh Perspectives on Women in Ministry, Zondervan eBook, release date 25/12/2012).

[10] James D.G. Dunn, 'Paul Was Talking Only About Households', *Church Times*, special supplement on women bishops, 18 January 2013, pp. 4-5.

[11] John Dickson, *Hearing Her Voice: A Case for Women Giving Sermons* (Fresh Perspectives on Women in Ministry, Zondervan eBook, release date 25/12/2012).

confirm this pattern for the relation between husbands and wives. But certain New Testament texts also indicate that this pattern is expected to extend from a household context to 'the household of God'; that is, from genetic families to local church families. These texts suggest *at least* that the role of overseer/elder should be taken by a man in the household of God, just as a husband should take the primary leadership and teaching role within his own family.

The scope of this argument is hence deliberately limited. There is much more one could say on how the complementarity of men and women should affect roles and relations beyond the role of overseer/elder in church families, and beyond that into society more generally. However, the particular egalitarian claim being addressed here is that ministry roles within church families should *never* be dependent on gender. The single counter-example of the role of overseer/elder being permanently restricted to men is sufficient to disprove this claim.

But the focus of this study is not negative – merely on restriction and prohibition. We shall see throughout that the Scriptures positively affirm and encourage the ministry of women. From the beginning, the ministry of women is emphasised as necessary and essential to the task in the world God has given his people to do. With it, the church is shown to be vibrant and growing. Without it, the church is severely impeded. Complementarians have sometimes wrongly marginalised or downplayed the ministry of women (although there are plenty of examples of good practice too). However, we shall also see that the ministry of women is intended to function according to the pattern of gender complementarity. Wives are expected to conduct their service and ministry in constructive partnership with their husbands, a partnership in which the husband has leadership responsibility. Not all women are wives, of course, but the same overall pattern should be visible in church families – in 'the household of God'. And these asymmetric, ordered gender patterns established by God are a *good thing*. They are nothing to be ashamed of. When they are working well, they facilitate effective ministry – part of the good order by which the church of the living God acts as a 'pillar and bulwark of the truth' (1 Timothy 3:15). They are indeed themselves means through which complementary truths about Jesus are displayed to the world. Hence the title of this study: *positive* complementarianism.

2. The Creation in Genesis 1-3

So much has been written on the first three chapters of Genesis that one might well wonder whether there is anything more to say. Nevertheless, it may still be that there is, since so many studies on these chapters have ripped them out of both their historical context and their literary setting in the book of Genesis as whole. The first of these dangers is now well recognised; the second much less so. Most readers of Genesis now recognize that it was written in and to an ancient near east context (at least in part) to guard against certain kinds of idolatry and as a polemic against alternative origin stories. However, awareness of the *literary* context of Genesis 1-3 remains neglected. Very few studies properly acknowledge the literary function of these chapters in the book of Genesis. Reading Genesis 1-3 in the context of the whole book helps us to give these chapters their proper weight. It should lead us to recognize that the heart of the book does not lie here in its opening, but later in the book – in the Abrahamic cycle running from chapters 12 to 25. Taking the book as a whole, the overall purpose of Genesis would seem to be to evoke in its readers an Abrahamic-like faith in the LORD who, as Creator, can providentially keep his promises to spread blessing in a broken world. These promises are introduced and summarized in 12:1-3 at the beginning of the Abrahamic cycle. The Jacob and Joseph cycles running from chapter 25 to the end of the book then run with this central purpose, showing the line of promise begun in Abraham surviving to successive generations against extraordinary odds. If a response to these promises lies at the heart of the book, then we can expect the opening chapters to be setting up the situation where the *need* for promise of spreading blessing becomes clear.

Our particular concern here is the relationship between men and women in this background material. What we shall find is that there are three points early on in the Genesis narrative where this relationship is especially highlighted. The first highlights the common role of men and women in the original plan to fill the world with blessing (Genesis 1); the second highlights their partnership as distinctly male and female, working together to fulfil that plan (Genesis 2); and the third highlights the dysfunctional relationship that follows the subversion of the plan through sin – as the world begins to fill not with life and blessing, but with sin and death.

Commentators have often noted the careful literary structure of Genesis 1-3. We shall here follow the structures suggested in Henri Blocher's study *In the Beginning*. This takes 1:2-31 as two panels, with three days of separation to create spaces (1:3-13) followed by three days of filling those spaces (1:14-31), followed by a final day of rest (2:1-3).[1] The second creation narrative, which runs from 2:4-3:24, seems to follow a concentric structure, with the eating of the fruit at the centre:[2]

> A 2:5-17 God acting. Man placed alone to work garden. Warning of death given.
>
> B 2:18-25 God acting. Man has minor role. Woman created second, as helper.
>
> C 3:1-5 Dialogue: Snake and woman.
>
> D 3:6-8 Woman and man acting: fruit eaten.
>
> C' 3:9-13 Dialogue: God and man; God and woman.
>
> B' 3:14-19 God acting. Sentence passed, including male-female conflict
>
> A' 3:20-24 God acting. Man (and woman) driven out of garden. Access to tree of life denied.

2.1. Genesis 1:1–2:3

> [26] Then God said, 'Let us make humankind in our image, according to our likeness; and let them have dominion over the fish of the sea, and over the birds of the air, and over the cattle, and over all the wild animals of the earth, and over every creeping thing that creeps upon the earth.' [27] So God created humankind in his image, in the image of God he created them; male and female he created them. [28] God blessed them, and God said to them, 'Be fruitful and multiply, and fill the earth and subdue it; and have dominion over the fish of the sea and over the birds of the air and over every living thing that moves upon the earth.' (Genesis 1:26-28 NRSV)

---

[1] Henri Blocher, *In the Beginning: the Opening Chapters of Genesis* (Leicester: IVP, 1984), pp. 54-55.
[2] Blocher, *In the Beginning*, pp. 28-29.

Day Six of Genesis 1 describes the filling of the land created on Day Three. However, it might be better to say that it describes the *beginning* of that process. That is, although the creation can be declared 'very good' at the end of the day (1:31), it is also unfinished. Humanity is created to complete the process. God commands the man and woman to be fruitful and multiply, and *thus* the earth will be filled. God creates a reflection of his image in humanity, that image then multiplies and fills the earth. As it does so, the man and the woman display God's character of loving rule over the rest of creation, replicating on a smaller scale the loving rule he has over the creation as a whole. As they multiply, spreading his image, the process envisaged seems to be rather like the hope expressed later in the biblical story that 'the earth will be filled with the knowledge of the glory of the LORD, as the waters cover the sea' (Habakkuk 2:14; cf. Isaiah 11:9).

In order to multiply, humanity is made male and female. And as the image of God multiplies and fills the earth, it is explicit from verse 27 that the both male and female equally bear that image.

2.2. *Genesis 2:4–25*

> [15] The LORD God took the man and put him in the Garden of Eden to till it and keep it. [16] And the LORD God commanded the man, 'You may freely eat of every tree of the garden; [17] but of the tree of the knowledge of good and evil you shall not eat, for in the day that you eat of it you shall die.'
>
> [18] Then the LORD God said, 'It is not good that the man should be alone; I will make him a helper as his partner.' (2:15-18 NRSV)

It does seem that the creation of humanity described in Genesis 1:27 and the creation described in 2:4-25 are intended to be equal but complementary accounts of the same event, serving different functions. Of the two, the Genesis 2 account is closer to straightforward narrative. It follows a conventional story-telling pattern, setting up issues and problems and then showing them resolved as the narrative unfolds. As the chapter opens, there is a problem: no plants on the land (2:5). This is solved by the Lord God sending rain and forming a man to work the ground and take care of it (2:6-7, 15). There is a further problem, caused by the man being alone in the task he has been given (2:18a). So the Lord God makes him 'a helper as his partner' (2:18b, 20 NRSV): a woman (2:22-23).

It is sometimes claimed that the 'man' in Genesis 2:5-20 is not gendered until the making of the woman in 2:21-22. Two different words are used: *adam* (formed out of the ground, *adamah*) and *iysh*. It is argued that an ungendered *adam* falls asleep in verse 21 and then wakes up as two gendered beings: an *iysh* (man or husband) and an *ishshai* (woman or wife). But the verses do not read so straightforwardly. *After* the woman is made, verse 22 ends by saying that the Lord God 'brought her to the *adam*'. Verse 25 reads, 'the two were naked, *adam* and his wife...' There is no suggestion in the text that the *adam* of verses 5-20 is different from the distinctly male *adam* in verses 22 and 25.

So there is a sequence, an order, in the creation of the man and the woman in Genesis 2. The question is: why? What does this signify or imply?

Consider first the man when he is alone, before the forming of the woman. While alone, he is given the task of working and caring for the land in the garden (2:15). Then the Lord God says, 'It is not good that the man should be alone; I will make him a helper as his partner'. The very first thing implied by this sequence of creation is that the woman is *necessary, essential,* for the man. He is inadequate on his own. He needs a helper. Certainly there is more to the relationship between the man and the woman than partnership in the task of working the garden. Nevertheless, this partnership in a given task does seem to be one of the emphases of the Genesis account.

The NRSV translation at this point is 'a helper as his partner'. A word-for-word translation would be something like 'a helper like-opposite-him'. Much of the discussion on gender roles in Genesis has focussed on this phrase, to the exclusion of the surrounding narrative. But perhaps there is only a limited amount one can infer from it. On its own, to be 'like-opposite-him' could be taken in either an egalitarian sense (something like an exact 'mirror image') *or* in a complemenatarian sense (equal but different). The word helper (*ezer*) is most commonly used of God in the Hebrew Bible.[3] The Lord is a helper in the task and role he has given his people. Here, the woman is formed to be a helper in the task the Lord God has given the man. Egalitarians are right to infer that she cannot therefore be lesser than the man, any more than the LORD is lesser than his people. Nevertheless, the term

---

[3] Exodus 18:4; Deuteronomy 33:7, 29; Psalms 20:3, 115:9-11; 121:2; 124:8; 146:5; Daniel 11:34.

does imply an order, an asymmetry, in the relationship between the woman and the man. *She* helps *him* in the task *he* has been given (for them both to do), not the other way round.

So the woman is a helper for the man in the work of the garden. But more than that: it is also implied that the woman is to be a *hearer* – a hearer of the word given to the man. It is to the man while alone that the 'rule' of the garden is given: that he may eat from any tree but the tree of the knowledge of good and evil (2:16-17). By the beginning of Genesis 3, it is apparent in the dialogue between the woman and the serpent that the woman knows this warning. From whom did she learn it? The narrative sequence implies: from the man. It was his leadership responsibility to draw the woman as a helper into their combined task, and this meant teaching her the God-given boundaries given to him before her creation. When the woman rejects the word of God given through the man for the word given by the serpent, this pattern is subverted. If anything, *she* teaches *the man* to break the commandment, and he complies (3:6; cf. 3:17). She fails in her role as helper. But, more significantly, *the man fails*. He fails in his God-given role and responsibility, which encompasses both his own behaviour and that of the woman to whom he was to pass on the command. Hence he is called to account first in 3:9.

Drawing this all together, we may say that the while the woman *equally* bears the image of God (1:27), and is *essential* to the task the Lord God gives humanity to do (2:18), we can nonetheless conclude that it is the man who is given what we would normally call the leadership role in the partnership. The word 'hierarchy' is probably not appropriate for their relationship, since that is often taken to imply a difference in worth or value, which we are insisting is not the case here. But it does seem appropriate to say that the man is given a responsible authority within the task jointly given to them both. The relation of man and woman to the task is certainly not described as symmetric.

This conclusion – that the order or sequence of creation (man first, then woman) was intended to imply leadership and authority in the partnership – would most likely have been quickly assumed by the first readers of Genesis. Later in the book we are reminded of the culturally accepted importance of the role of the *firstborn* in ancient families. More often than not, it is the failure of the firstborn that is highlighted (as in Esau and Reuben). Nonetheless, the writer of Genesis seems to take it as well-accepted that the firstborn played a particular role in the family, with certain responsibilities. For example, Reuben seems aware in Genesis 37 of his responsibility to restrain his brothers, and in 42:22 we see his awareness that he has failed in that responsibility. In such a culture, a natural implication from the man being created first in Genesis 2 would be that the man would have a similar role and responsibility. There would have to be something explicit in the text to cancel this assumption. But there is no such corrective in Genesis 2. Rather, as we have argued, the narrative sequence supports the claim that the man is given a leadership role in the partnership.

2.3. Genesis 3

> [16] To the woman he said, 'I will greatly increase your pangs in childbearing; in pain you shall bring forth children, yet your desire shall be for your husband, and he shall rule over you.'
>
> [17] And to the man he said, 'Because you have listened to the voice of your wife, and have eaten of the tree about which I commanded you, 'You shall not eat of it,' cursed is the ground because of you; in toil you shall eat of it all the days of your life...' (3:16-17 NRSV)

Some egalitarian readings of Genesis 1-3 have to claim that any asymmetry in the relation between man and woman appears for the very first time here, at Genesis 3:16. *This* is the point at which the desire of one party to rule over the other enters the story, and not before. 'Your desire shall be for your husband,' says the LORD. The word 'desire' is used negatively in 4:7, where the LORD says to Cain, '[...] sin is lurking at the door; its *desire* is for you, but you must master it' (NRSV). This suggests that the woman will want to overcome the man in some way. Against this, she is told 'and he shall rule over you'. In this reading, such 'rule' is a new thing; something that wasn't there before. On this reading, the crisis of Genesis 3 thus introduces an asymmetry between the woman and the man for the first time: an asymmetry expressed as a power struggle, a fight for supremacy. When humanity is made new in Christ, the implication is then that we should then renounce any such asymmetry.

Much of this we can agree with. Something new does happen at Genesis 3:16 – a 'desire' to overcome and a kind of 'rule' that wasn't there before. However, rather than proclaiming a new asymmetry emerging out of symmetry, it makes better sense in the context to take it as a *distorted asymmetry arising out of the attempted reversal of an existing asymmetry*. The sentence given by the LORD God in response to what has happened restores the correct *direction* of the order and asymmetry between man and woman. But because of the sinfulness of the parties, the result is *conflict* within in a dysfunctional, unharmonious relationship.

Several considerations in the narrative sequence point in this direction. We have already argued for a benign asymmetry between man and woman implied by the order of creation in Genesis 2. The creation order is then subverted when the serpent (a creature over which both man and woman should have dominion) teaches the woman and the woman then teaches the man (3:1-8). Having exposed what has happened (3:9-13), the LORD God then passes sentence in response to this subversion (3:14-19). We see this in Genesis 3:17, where the LORD God reminds the man of the reason for the current crisis: 'Because you have listened to the voice of your wife, and have eaten of the tree about which I commanded *you* [...]'. That is, a significant component of the man's failure has been a failure of loving leadership. Likewise, the woman is also punished for what she has done, which includes living within the dysfunctional relationship of 3:16. The structure of Genesis 2-3 suggests a connection between the order of the relations described in 2:18-25 and 3:14-19. These sections mirror one another in the structure. What remains the same is the direction of order: the man remains the leader; the woman remains the one led. But now on-going sin means she tends to resist this direction of order ('your desire shall be for your husband'), while he will tend to respond aggressively rather than lovingly – 'he shall rule over you'. The result is dysfunctional conflict in place of harmonious partnership.

2.4. *The wider literary function of Genesis 1-3 in Genesis as a whole*

There are no *direct, explicit* ethical implications for the relations between men and women or husbands and wives drawn out in the text of Genesis 1-3 in the rest of the book. It is only when we turn to the New Testament texts such as 1 Corinthians 11:8 and 1 Timothy 2:13-14 that we find a direct appeal to these chapters in support of certain ethical injunctions, and we shall consider these below. But it is still worth asking what function the ordered asymmetry of Genesis 2 serves within the confines of the book of Genesis alone. If it *can* be shown to serve some function, then it is less likely to be the spurious invention of stubborn conservatives. And a possible answer may lie in Genesis 16, at the heart of the Abrahamic cycle – which we have already argued is at the heart of the book. The links between Genesis 16 and Genesis 3 are very strong. Sarai thinks the LORD has kept children from her (16:2), much as the woman thought the fruit was being kept from her (3:6). She takes the initiative, commanding her husband, much as the woman did in the garden. He complies submissively, just as the man in the garden did. It is clear in the narrative that this is a major backwards step for Abram, resulting in thirteen years of silence before the LORD calls him back (16:16-17:1). The implication could be that as Abraham grows in faith and in his walk before the LORD in the way of blessing, he needs to renounce the weak leadership of his forefather Adam. Rather, he should have been leading the way in trusting God's promise, and leading and teaching Sarai to do likewise.

If this is right, then the kind of leadership the Abraham narrative implicitly commends for the person of faith is emphatically not a Genesis 3:16 kind of leadership. Both complementarians and egalitarians should then be able to agree that faith should result in *radical change* in the relations between men and women, husbands and wives. Biblical complementarianism is not a defence of the status quo. But Genesis suggests that faith should not only curtail the aggressive, reactive 'rule' implied by Genesis 3:16, it should also correct the weak leadership exhibited by Adam in 3:6 and Abram in 16:2-4.

2.5. *Conclusions from Genesis 1-3 in its literary context*

From the three points early on in the Genesis narrative where the relationship between men and women is especially highlighted we can draw three main conclusions, one from each of the first chapters. From Genesis 1, men and women have a common role and status in God's plan to fill the world with blessing. From Genesis 2, they are nevertheless distinctly male and female within that partnership, as they work together to fulfil that plan. We have argued for a benign asymmetry in this relationship, with the first-created man given a leadership responsibility comparable to that of the firstborn in an ancient family. Finally, from Genesis 3, when God's plans are subverted by rebellion, the consequences of that rebellion are felt within the partnership, which becomes hostile and dysfunctional. All this provides the background to a failure of faith by Abram in Genesis 16. The implication is that the man of faith should *lead* in faith within the marriage partnership, renouncing the weak leadership of Adam.

We shall be arguing below that as men and women become united to Christ by faith, they should be bringing reconciliation to the conflict of 3:16, thus returning their relations to the pattern of Genesis 2. The result should be something beautiful – an equal but ordered partnership much like that between two ballroom dancers. Hence the cover of this study. The partnership between two ballroom dancers functions and succeeds because one of them takes the lead. However, his purpose in leading is not to magnify himself. His concern is direction and coordination – as is his partner's, as she responds co-operatively. If anything, the male lead is more concerned to magnify his female partner, making *her* the centre of attention. Likewise in marriage, where husbands are called to emulate the love of Christ to the church – giving himself for her, *to present her to himself as a radiant church* (Ephesians 5:25-27). Marriage is a dance to display the character and glory of Christ.

3. The New Testament Teaching

3.1. Galatians 3:28

> [27] As many of you as were baptized into Christ have clothed yourselves with Christ. [28] There is no longer Jew or Greek, there is no longer slave or free, there is no longer male and female; for all of you are one in Christ Jesus. [29] And if you belong to Christ, then you are Abraham's offspring, heirs according to the promise. (Galatians 3:27-29 NRSV)

As Paul explains that the purpose of the Mosaic Law was to act as a custodian until the time of Christ, exposing sin as legal transgression, he outlines the benefits to those who have been freed from its slavery and baptized into Christ. Clothed with Christ, united in him, divisions created by sin and Law are broken down – uniting Jew and Gentile, slave and free, male and female. In Christ, the conflict of Genesis 3:16 is resolved.

This is obviously a key text for egalitarians, and should be for complementarians too. We can rejoice that in Christ the mutual image-bearing of Genesis 1:26 is declared to be restored in the justified community.

Some egalitarians claim that Galatians 3:28 declares an entirely new order of relations between men and women. Men and women should not, having been united to Christ, return to the pattern of Genesis 2 (which these interpreters regard, acknowledging the asymmetry we observed above, to be steeped in 'patriarchalism'). Instead, Galatians 3:28 declares that *all* gender distinctions are broken down, including those of Genesis 2. But this is surely inferring far too much from a single clause and disregarding its context. Paul's specific concern in Galatians is to answer the question, 'Who receives the blessings of the Abrahamic promises?' His answer is: anyone who is united by faith to Christ, whether they be Jew or Gentile, slave or free, male or female. In Galatians 3, Paul is not addressing issues of detailed application as he does in the so-called 'household codes' elsewhere. To be equal beneficiaries of the Abrahamic promises in Christ has, on its own, no *detailed* implications for how being 'in Christ' as a man might differ from being 'in Christ' as a woman. For the detail, we have to look elsewhere, as we shall do below. For the moment, it will suffice to say that just as the equal status of men and women as image-bearers (Genesis 1:26) is compatible with an asymmetry in their relationship (Genesis 2), so it is with the equality of men and women in Christ.

3.2. Women in the Gospels and Acts

> [10] Now it was Mary Magdalene, Joanna, Mary the mother of James, and the other women with them who told this to the apostles. [11] But these words seemed to them an idle tale, and they did not believe them. (Luke 24:10-11 NRSV)

If the gospel declares the destruction of sinful distinctions and conflict between men and women in Christ, is then not surprising to see this expressed in the Gospel accounts. One of the very early witnesses in Luke's Gospel to the great new thing God is doing is of course from a woman. At the centre of the *Magnificat*, Mary proclaims: *He has brought down the powerful from their thrones, and lifted up the lowly* (Luke 1:52 NRSV). This begins a prominent theme in the Gospel as Jesus works out his Servant ministry 'to bring good news to the poor [...] to proclaim release to the captives and recovery of sight to the blind, to let the oppressed go free, to proclaim the year of the Lord's favour' (Luke 4:18-19 NRSV). Beginning with Mary, Jesus' ministry draws women into God's plans and purposes in manner which itself testifies to how the gospel speaks to the humble rather than the self-sufficient or proud. Significantly, women are the first witnesses to Jesus' resurrection, and humble the male disciples who at first don't believe them (Luke 24:10-11).

The importance of women in the gospel ministry of the early church remains a significant emphasis in the book of Acts. Perhaps most striking here is the combined ministry of Priscilla and Aquilla in Acts 18. Priscilla and Aquilla were travel companions of Paul between Corinth and Ephesus (Acts 18:18-19). In Ephesus, when they heard Apollos speak in the Synagogue, 'they took him aside and explained the Way of God to him more accurately' (18:26 NRSV). We might say: they 'filled him in' on the way of God. In this context at least, a woman explaining something to a man is implicitly commended by the narrative.

3.3. Romans 16

> I commend to you our sister Phoebe, a deacon of the church at Cenchreae, [2] so that you may welcome her in the Lord as is

> fitting for the saints, and help her in whatever she may require from you, for she has been a benefactor of many and of myself as well.
>
> ³ Greet Prisca and Aquila, who work with me in Christ Jesus, ⁴ and who risked their necks for my life, to whom not only I give thanks, but also all the churches of the Gentiles.
>
> ⁵ Greet also the church in their house.
>
> Greet my beloved Epaenetus, who was the first convert in Asia for Christ.
>
> ⁶ Greet Mary, who has worked very hard among you.
>
> ⁷ Greet Andronicus and Junia, my relatives who were in prison with me; they are prominent among the apostles, and they were in Christ before I was. (Romans 16:1-7 NRSV)

The commendation and greetings in Romans 16, expressing the mutual love extending between Christians in different places, are remarkable for the number of women Paul mentions: Pheobe, Prisca, Mary, Junia, Trypanaena, Tryphosa, Persis, Rufus's mother and Julia. Pheobe may well have been the bearer of the letter. Mary, Tryphaena, Tryphosa and Persis are described as 'working hard', a word Paul uses of his own ministry in a number of places.[1] Paul does not say precisely what they have been working hard at, but we cannot doubt that their labour in ministry was vital and valuable.

So Paul gladly declares the unity of men and women in Christ Jesus, and celebrates the partnership of men and women in ministry. Nevertheless, in the next two passages, we shall see him explicitly defending gender complementarity in marriage.

3.4. 1 Corinthians 11:2-16

> ² I commend you because you remember me in everything and maintain the traditions just as I handed them on to you. ³ But I want you to understand that Christ is the head of every man, and the husband is the head of his wife, and God is the head of Christ. ⁴ Any man who prays or prophesies with something on his head disgraces his head, ⁵ but any woman who prays or

---

[1] 1 Corinthians 15:10; Galatians 4:11; Philippians 2:16; Colossians 1:29; 1 Timothy 4:10.

> prophesies with her head unveiled disgraces her head— it is one and the same thing as having her head shaved. ⁶ For if a woman will not veil herself, then she should cut off her hair; but if it is disgraceful for a woman to have her hair cut off or to be shaved, she should wear a veil. ⁷ For a man ought not to have his head veiled, since he is the image and reflection of God; but woman is the reflection of man. ⁸ Indeed, man was not made from woman, but woman from man. ⁹ Neither was man created for the sake of woman, but woman for the sake of man. ¹⁰ For this reason a woman ought to have a symbol of authority on her head, because of the angels. (1 Corinthians 11:2-10 NRSV)

Earlier in the letter, Paul has been exhorting the Gentile Christians in Corinth to flee sexual immorality but instead to glorify God with their bodies (1 Corinthians 4:18-7:40). Since 8:1, he has been helping them to avoid association with the other characteristically Gentile vice: idolatry. And in 1 Corinthians 11 he then turns to more positive teaching about good order in the gathered community. Men and women (in particular, wives) should wear or not wear on their heads whatever accurately communicates in Corinthian culture the God-given distinction between them.

Although this is often considered a difficult passage (and we do not really have space in this study to do justice to it), it is clear enough to see what Paul means by 'the head of woman is man' (1 Corinthians 11:3). And we must insist that 'head' does indeed have connotations of authority here.[2] The line of interpretation that takes head to mean something like 'source' is very hard to substantiate. We should also note that it would leave Paul teaching an Arian, subordinationist doctrine, with God as the 'source' of Christ. What is more, such a reading results in an argument that is very hard to make any sense of. Paul presumably uses 'head' as a metaphor in verse 3 because he is just about to teach the Corinthian husbands and wives what they should do with their physical *heads*. And that teaching confirms the meaning of the metaphor: wives should on their *heads* wear 'a symbol of authority' (11:10). We can reach

---

[2] This is in line with most recent commentaries. Take, for example, Roy Ciampa and Brian Rosner, *The First Letter to the Corinthians*, Pillar NT Commentary (Nottingham: Apollos, 2012), p.509, 'In this context the word almost certainly refers to one with authority over another'. There is a detailed discussion of the various options in Anthony Thiselton, *The First Epistle to the Corinthians*, NIGTC (Carlise: Paternoster, 2000), pp.812-22.

this conclusion without having to decide *precisely* what it signified for a woman to cover or veil her head in Corinthian culture, or to speculate on why certain women had chosen not to do so in the Corinthian churches.³ Paul is *at least* saying that husbands have leadership authority over their wives (11:3), and he is saying this on the basis of the creation order of Genesis 2 (11:8-9). This is however compatible with her freedom to pray and prophesy in church meetings (11:5), and does not contradict the mutual dependence of men and women (11:11-12).

3.5. *Ephesians 5:8-6:9*

²¹ Be subject to one another out of reverence for Christ.

²² Wives, be subject to your husbands as you are to the Lord. ²³ For the husband is the head of the wife just as Christ is the head of the church, the body of which he is the Saviour. ²⁴ Just as the church is subject to Christ, so also wives ought to be, in everything, to their husbands.

²⁵ Husbands, love your wives, just as Christ loved the church and gave himself up for her... (Ephesians 5:21-25 NRSV)

As Paul works out the practical implications of leading 'a life worthy of the calling to which you have been called' (Ephesians 4:1), he exhorts the Ephesian Christians not to be 'drunk with wine [...] but be filled with the Spirit' (5:18). This is then expanded in a sequence covering singing (5:19), giving thanks (5:20) and ending with submitting to one another (5:21). This is then further applied to different kinds of relationship within the body of Christ, beginning with wives and husbands.

Ephesians 5:22-33 does seem to be one of the places in the Bible where some sort of gender complementarity between husbands and wives is most clearly expressed. It is a very hard for egalitarians to avoid the asymmetry here. It is true that there is the general statement in verse 21: *be subject to one another out of reverence for Christ*. But I am persuaded that this is then spelt out and qualified for first wives and then husbands in what follows in *different* ways. How should wives be

---

³ Or indeed to work out what Paul means by 'because of the angels' (11:10)! Possibly, Paul is again encouraging the Corinthians to think about glorifying God by alluding to the Septuagint version of Psalm 8, where humanity is 'made a little lower than angels and crowned with glory and honour' (Psalm 8:6 LXX; 8:5 ENG).

subject to their husbands out of reverence for Christ? The answer is in verse 22: be subject to your husbands *as you are to the Lord*. How should husbands be subject to their wives out of reverence for Christ? The answer is in verse 25: be subject to your wives as an expression of self-giving love, *just as Christ loved the church*.

There is one principle (verse 21), worked out in asymmetric but complementary ways according to gender. As Mary Kassian noted (see above), the complementarity between husbands and wives displays complementary truths about Jesus.

Whether this complementarity should extend beyond husbands and wives to other male-female relations we have yet to discuss.

3.6. 1 Peter 3:1-7

> Wives, in the same way, accept the authority of your husbands, so that, even if some of them do not obey the word, they may be won over without a word by their wives' conduct, ² when they see the purity and reverence of your lives. ³ Do not adorn yourselves outwardly by braiding your hair, and by wearing gold ornaments or fine clothing; ⁴ rather, let your adornment be the inner self with the lasting beauty of a gentle and quiet spirit, which is very precious in God's sight. ⁵ It was in this way long ago that the holy women who hoped in God used to adorn themselves by accepting the authority of their husbands. ⁶ Thus Sarah obeyed Abraham and called him lord. You have become her daughters as long as you do what is good and never let fears alarm you. (1 Peter 3:1-6 NRSV)

As Peter expands on what it means to live 'honourably among the Gentiles, so that, [...] they may see your honourable deeds and glorify God when he comes to judge' (1 Peter 2:12 NRSV), he turns from general statements (2:13-17), to slaves (2:18-25) and then to wives and husbands (3:1-7). Wives are instructed to 'accept the authority of' (NRSV) or 'be subject to' (ESV) their husbands. The same word is used in 3:22 to describe how angels, authorities and powers have become subject to the exalted Jesus Christ.

These verses are worth considering briefly for a number of reasons. To begin with, they remind us that the explicit teaching on husbands and wives in the NT does not just come from Paul. Second, they clearly commend an asymmetric relationship between wives and husbands. True, the kind of marriage Peter has in view is at first between a believing wife and an unbelieving husband. Perhaps then it doesn't apply to marriages between believers? But Peter goes on to draw on Abraham and Sarah as a positive example (1 Peter 3:5-6) and then goes on to address *believing* husbands (1 Peter 3:7).[4] But a third reason for considering this passage is that it allows us to address a very common argument for the egalitarian view, based on its proximity to Peter's teaching on slaves obeying their masters (1 Peter 2:18-25).

This argument begins by rightly observing that in the Greco-Roman world, good social order was widely considered to include three elements:[5]

1. Wives submitting to husbands (and women subordinate to men in general)
2. Children obeying parents
3. Slaves obeying masters

If these three things were in place, it was assumed that good social order would follow. It is also right to note that in order not to bring the gospel into disrepute, the NT churches were encouraged to conform to this pattern. Indeed, it is striking that two of the so-called 'household codes' in the NT have this three-fold pattern (Ephesians 5:22-6:9; Colossians 3:18-25). 1 Peter 2:13-3:7 covers slaves-masters and wives-husbands. 1 Timothy 5:1-6:2 and Titus 2:2-10 cover men and women of different ages and slaves. The argument then goes on to suggest that just as when the unjust social institution of slavery disappeared, former slaves were no longer required to obey former masters with 'fear and trembling', so it is with the submission of wives to husbands.

However, this argument is hard to substantiate. Peter makes it very clear that he understands the potential injustice slaves may well face in relations with their masters:

Slaves, accept the authority of your masters with all deference,

---

[4] Why does Peter describe wives here as 'the weaker vessel'? The most likely explanation is that by the husband assuming a leadership authority within the marriage, the wife automatically becomes the more vulnerable partner. The husband could selfishly exploit this power advantage. Peter calls them not to, but rather to treat their wives with proper respect as co-heirs of the gift of life (cf. Galatians 3:28).

[5] Craig S. Keener, *Paul, Women & Wives: Marriage and Women's Ministry in the Letters of Paul* (Peabody, Mass.: Hendrickson, 1992), pp. 145-46.

not only those who are kind and gentle but also those who are harsh. ¹⁹ For it is a credit to you if, being aware of God, you endure pain while suffering unjustly. (1 Peter 2:18-19 NRSV)

Even if the situation is unjust, behaving rightly and well is a witness to a faith in the God who judges justly, a faith which follows the example of Jesus as he faced injustice.

However, the call to wives to 'accept the authority of' (NRSV) their own husbands is not supported by Peter in the same way. Rather, it is presented as something which *adorns* the wife, displaying a God-honouring beauty (1 Peter 3:4). The example Peter then draws on is not a wife honouring an unjust, unbelieving husband, but Sarah accepting the authority of Abraham (3:6). As we noted above, Abraham and Sarah were called to express a humanity in which the creation order was renewed by the promise of God's blessing. This they did in a faltering and haphazard fashion – but in this instance Peter is suggesting they got it right, and that Sarah's example should be followed. It seems clear that Peter thought the principle to be an enduring one (rather than one that would change with changing social structures), much like the rightness of children obeying their parents (Ephesians 6:1-3; Colossians 3:20).

3.7. *Leadership in the Synoptic Gospels – Matt 20:20-28 et par.*

²⁵ But Jesus called them to him and said, 'You know that the rulers of the Gentiles lord it over them, and their great ones are tyrants over them. ²⁶ It will not be so among you; but whoever wishes to be great among you must be your servant, ²⁷ and whoever wishes to be first among you must be your slave; ²⁸ just as the Son of Man came not to be served but to serve, and to give his life a ransom for many.' (Matthew 20:25-28 NRSV)

We have looked at one set of NT texts which affirm the unity of male and female as co-heirs of blessing in Christ and which describe and commend the role and value of women for gospel ministry in the NT community. And we have seen another set of texts which exhort a visible, worked-out gender complementarity between husbands and wives, with husbands given leadership authority. One temptation is to separate these into two opposing strands of teaching and claim, for example, that the first strand is the dominant trajectory of the early church, while the second was fading away. But this will not do for consistent Anglicans, who maintain that it is not lawful for the Church to 'so expound one place of Scripture, that it be repugnant to another' (Article 20 of the 39 Articles).

But to see that there is no logical contradiction between equality in a marriage and one party (the husband) having leadership authority, we turn here, to Matthew 20:25-28. It is a passage that ostensibly has no mention of gender. However, it does tell us much about the Christian understanding of *leadership*. It may be that some arguments for egalitarianism implicitly depend upon a false understanding of Christian leadership.

Suppose that it was thought that within a leader-led relationship, the leader is naturally understood to have a higher value or status on account of his or her authority within that relationship. In Matthew 20:25, this corresponds to a 'Gentile' understanding of leadership, where rulers 'lord it over' their subjects. (This is the same word as in the Greek version of Genesis 1:28 used to describe humanity's dominion over the creation. To 'lord it over' someone is thus to treat them like an animal relative to yourself.) Under this understanding of leadership, if certain leadership roles are restricted to men, then it is easy to see how this might be taken to imply that men therefore have the higher value or status. One way to address this misconception is thus to allow equal access to leadership roles across the genders. The relationship between gender and leadership then implies nothing about gender and status.

However, Jesus makes it clear that this is a *false* understanding of leadership. The Christian understanding of leadership is that involves assuming if anything a *lower* status – that of a servant. The servant-work of Jesus does transform leadership roles – and should therefore transform the dysfunctional situation of husbands 'ruling over' wives in Genesis 3:16. If we follow Mary Kassian (see above) in understanding the term 'patriarchal' to refer to cultures or societies distorted by men leading women like 'the rulers of the Gentiles,' lording it over them, then Jesus' teaching is anti-patriarchal. But in speaking against such leadership, Jesus is not doing away with leadership roles. It should be possible, following him, to lead in such a servant-hearted way that does not imply anything about relative value or status. The restriction of leadership authority to husbands is therefore not *automatically* in conflict with the equality of husband and wife before God. Likewise, the restriction of other leadership roles to men would not be *automatically* in conflict with the equality of men and women before God.

3.8. *1 Corinthians 12:12-31*

> ¹⁵ If the foot should say, "Because I am not a hand, I do not belong to the body," that would not make it any less a part of the body. [...] ¹⁸ But as it is, God arranged the members in the body, each one of them, as he chose.

As with Matthew 20:25-28 above, this is not a passage which deals explicitly with relations between men and women, or husbands and wives. However, like the Matthew text, it may well be relevant in addressing some of the concerns underlying the egalitarian position.

The complementarian view claims that certain leadership roles in the 'body' of a church family are given by God to men only. To people living in an egalitarian age and culture, this seems unjust and unfair. Shouldn't those denied such roles by their gender rightly say, 'because I cannot be such a leader, I am not fully a part of the body'? A comparison with 1 Corinthians 12 would suggest not.

To an extent, egalitarians would agree with the general principle. They do, after all, want to restrict leadership roles according to giftedness. But why exclude gender from giftedness? Isn't one's gender a very obvious and visible gift from God?

3.9. *Acts and Romans 16 revisited*

So what about gender and leadership roles outside of marriage, and especially within the wider Christian communities? We saw above the importance of women in the gospel ministry of the early church affirmed as a significant emphasis in the book of Acts. However, it is also apparent from the book of Acts that leadership roles and church-planting roles were exclusively taken by men. Women were not considered for the replacement for Judas in Acts 1:21-22, despite Mary Magdalene, for example, having both been with Jesus in his earthly ministry and having witnessed his resurrection. Every figure taking an overall leadership role in the church's mission as recounted in Acts is male (and Priscilla is not an exception). This is not disputed by writers arguing for the egalitarian view. Take Ian Paul, writing in a Grove Booklet in 2011:

> Women have prominent roles in Luke, but all the main figures

in the church's mission in Acts are men.[6]

He then quotes Robert Tannehill who, with many others, suggests that this 'reflects cultural resistance to women as witnesses [...] and in public roles, such as speakers'.[7] Ian Paul himself goes on to suggest that men in Acts assume primacy as witnesses because of their failure of faith in the Gospel story relative to women. They therefore testify more fully to the grace of God. However, he offers no biblical evidence for this view.

So was this distinction between the genders in Acts intended to be a temporary phenomenon – a concession to the cultural prejudices of the day, or a (temporary?) demonstration of the grace of God to faithless men? We can find no explicit suggestion along such lines in Acts or elsewhere in the New Testament. Indeed, we shall find the explicit teaching on gender distinction and leadership roles within the household of faith in the Pastoral Epistles points to a deeper, more enduring reason.

The evidence from Romans 16 does not overturn the basic claim that leadership roles and church-planting roles were exclusively taken by men. Phoebe is a servant or deacon, not an elder or overseer. There is a broad consensus that in using *prostatis* in Romans 16:2 Paul is describing her as helper, patron or benefactor – but nothing more than this. This is clear from the way the clause it appears in supports the previous sub-point. Paul says, in effect, '*Help* her... for she has also been *a helper* of many (including me)'.[8] Junia in Romans 16:7 may have 'prominent among the apostles' (although the translation 'noteworthy in the eyes of the apostles' seems more likely), but there is no positive evidence that she was a church-planter in her own right or had oversight over a local church or over local churches. She was not one of the Twelve, and someone can be sent – and hence 'an apostle' – in the NT without necessarily having such authority.

---

[6] Ian Paul, *Women and Authority: The Key Biblical Texts*, Grove Biblical Series B59, 2011, p.10.

[7] Robert Tannehill, *Luke* (Nashville: Abingdon, 1996), p.351.

[8] Steven Croft links the word to *proistamenos* in Romans 12:8, which is translated 'the leader' in the NRSV. Steven Croft, 'The Women of the Early Church', in Steven Croft and Paula Gooder (eds.), *Women and Men in Scripture and the Church: A Guide to the Key Issues* (Norwich: Canterbury Press, 2013), p.28. But I don't know of any wider scholarship which claims she had leadership authority over Paul. Any etymological connection between *prostatis* and *ho proistamevos* is pragmatically cancelled by its general usage and the context in Romans 16. (Likewise in English, we do not infer from the etymology of 'cupboard' that it must be a shelf for cups.)

So Romans 16 supports the claim (with which we wholeheartedly agree) that women played important, significant roles in the ministry and mission of the early church. But Romans 16 cannot be made to say more than this without a high level of speculation.

3.10. 1 Corinthians 14:34-35

> As in all the churches of the saints, [34] women should be silent in the churches. For they are not permitted to speak, but should be subordinate, as the law also says. [35] If there is anything they desire to know, let them ask their husbands at home. For it is shameful for a woman to speak in church. (1 Corinthians 14:33-35 NRSV)

Before turning to the Pastoral Epistles, we shall consider one more text, from 1 Corinthians 14:34-35. Paul is continuing to teach about good order in the gathered community. Having given instruction on when tongues-speakers should be silent (14:28), when givers of prophesy should be silent (14:30), Paul then turns to say something about when wives or women should be silent.

There have been some attempts to suggest that these verses were a later insertion by some particularly misogynist scribe. They do not seem to be essential to the flow of thought, and in a very few manuscripts appear in a different place. But every extant manuscript includes them, and we would expect more changes from such an over-enthusiastic scribe – removing or amending 11:5, for example, where Paul talks about wives or women being not at all silent as they pray and prophesy.

So what's going on here? With some others, Michael Bird suggests that Paul is talking about wives who inappropriately interrupt a word of prophesy to ask their husbands about it – or perhaps contradicting or shaming their husbands in other ways.[9] This is possible because the Greek for 'wives' is the same as the Greek for 'women'. The verses should thus read:

> As in all the churches of the saints,[34] *wives* should be silent in the churches. For they are not permitted to speak, but should be

---

[9] Michael Bird, *Bourgeois Babes*, section 'Woman and Silence', para 6. This follows the discussion in Ciampa and Rosner, *First Corinthians*, pp.718-730.

subordinate, as the law also says. ³⁵ If there is anything they desire to know, let them ask their husbands at home. For it is shameful for a *wife* to speak in church.

Wives 'should be subordinate, as the law also says'. Paul is possibly referring to the patriarchal narratives where, for example, Sarah shows respect to her husband (cf. 1 Peter 3:1-7 above). Or he may be referring to the relational pattern at the beginning of the Law, set in Genesis 2. Instead of speaking out of turn, Paul instructs, wives should ask their husbands at home, in a more appropriate setting (verse 35).

But the literary context may suggest a more specific situation: the weighing of prophesy. In 14:29, Paul says, 'Let two or three prophets speak, and let the others weigh what is said'. *If* the 'others' here are church leaders and church leadership is restricted to men, then this may explain the prohibition in verse 24. As the male leaders/elders weigh prophesy, wives should let them do so in silence. And if wives, then women in the congregation more generally. The prohibition may therefore be consistent with the restriction of leadership roles and the weighing of prophesy to men, even if it doesn't prove such a restriction. To *prove* such a restriction, we need to turn to the Pastoral Epistles.

4. New Testament: 1 Timothy and Titus

So far we have been reminded that men and women have equal status within the justified community (Galatians 3:28); Paul's gospel declared the image-bearing equality of Genesis 1:26 to be restored in Christ Jesus. Consequently, women are highly involved (in the Gospels), active (Acts) and valued (Romans 16) when it comes to gospel ministry. However, just as the equality of Genesis 1:26 was not contradicted by the implied gender differences of Genesis 2, so the equality of Galatians 3:28 is not contradicted by the apostolic teaching on gender distinctions in marriage. The apostolic teaching on marriages consistently maintains that husbands should lead the marriage partnership, and have the authority to do so, and wives should cooperate (1 Corinthians 11, Ephesians 5, 1 Peter 3:1-7). This does not contradict the assertion of equality, because in biblical understanding leadership is *servant* leadership (Matthew 20:20-28 *et par*) and submission, if appropriate, is highly valued. Leadership does not imply superiority and submission does not imply inferiority. Moreover, for different people to have different roles says nothing about their relative value or status – all are important (1 Corinthians 12). It follows that if it were true that there were a similar restriction of roles outside the context of marriage, then this would also not contradict the claim of equality.

The key question remains: *does* the New Testament teaching restrict certain roles outside marriage on the basis of gender? The practice of the early church seems to affirm the suggestion, and we have found no examples of women leading or planting churches in Acts or Romans 16, even if women were clearly actively and vibrantly involved in ministry of many kinds. We have also seen that 1 Corinthians 14 *perhaps* suggests that the weighing of prophesy in the church body was restricted to male leaders, with women expected to keep quiet during the process. But for more explicit teaching on gender and roles within the church household, we do need to turn to the Pastoral Epistles, beginning with 1 Timothy.

It is important to say again at this point that it is beyond the scope of this study to explore all the implications for male-female relations from 1 Timothy, across marriage, church and society. The aim here is rather to refute the claim that ministry roles within church families should *never* be dependent on gender. To refute this claim requires just one example of a role being permanently restricted to men.

The argument below is that 1 Timothy implies *at least* that the role of overseer/elder in the household of God should be taken by a man.

In 1 Timothy, Paul would seem to be addressing a church situation that has become inward focussed, full of in-fighting and competition, fuelled by false teaching, leaving the church body distracted from their main task as a proclaimer of the truth. Paul therefore gives Timothy instruction on how to redress the situation, helpfully summarizing his purpose in 1 Timothy 3:14-15:

> [14] I hope to come to you soon, but I am writing these instructions to you so that, [15] if I am delayed, you may know how one ought to behave in the household of God, which is the church of the living God, the pillar and bulwark of the truth. (1 Timothy 3:14-15 NRSV)

The letter to Titus is likewise written to address a situation on Crete being wrecked by false teaching and conduct (Titus 1:10-16). Part of the solution is for Titus to appoint elders in every town (1:5): an elder being godly man who has 'a firm grasp of the word that is trustworthy in accordance with the teaching, so that he may be able both to preach with sound doctrine and to refute those who contradict it' (1:9 NRSV).

Quite how to make the move from these quite specific historical settings to infer what is right more generally, and what is right in 21st Century England for example, is of course a huge issue – although it is not insurmountable. Our consideration above of Paul's teaching in 1 Corinthians 11 above raised the possibility that his instruction can be grounded in the order of creation and yet also have a culturally and historically specific application (such as: married women should wear veils while prophesying or praying). Likewise in 1 Timothy, there are culturally specific details. Men praying is associated with raised hands (2:8). Braided hair is associated with immodesty and wearing jewellery to lack of self-control (2:9). Are these associations always valid across all history and culture? It seems unlikely. Commentators are also correct to point out the specific historical circumstances of the Ephesian churches. These are churches infected by false teaching (1 Timothy 1), some of which seems to be linked to myths about the Creation (4:1-4). What's more, there are young widows causing trouble (5:11-15) – not getting married, and saying what they ought not to say. Paul suggests they should get married and bear children – which possibly connects with his comment about finding salvation through childbearing in 2:15.

However, having acknowledged the possibility, we should also leave open the possibility that 1 Timothy 2:12 is *not* culturally or historically specific. While an application peculiar to first century Ephesus is an *a priori* possibility and while, as we shall see, many interpretations of these verses claim this, I shall be arguing from both the detail of the verses and from their context in the letter a more general and enduring application.

There are two parts to this argument. The first is a negative argument, based on the prohibition of 1 Timothy 2:12. This covers much well-trodden ground and is fairly complex. The second is a much simpler positive argument, based on the wider context and purpose of the letter and, especially, on 1 Timothy 3 and Titus 1.

4.1. *1 Timothy 2:8-15 – an important but complex negative case for gender complementarity in church leadership roles*

> [8] I desire, then, that in every place the men should pray, lifting up holy hands without anger or argument; [9] also that the women should dress themselves modestly and decently in suitable clothing, not with their hair braided, or with gold, pearls, or expensive clothes, [10] but with good works, as is proper for women who profess reverence for God. [11] Let a woman learn in silence with full submission. [12] I permit no woman to teach or to have authority over a man; she is to keep silent. [13] For Adam was formed first, then Eve; [14] and Adam was not deceived, but the woman was deceived and became a transgressor. [15] Yet she will be saved through childbearing, provided they continue in faith and love and holiness, with modesty. (1 Timothy 2:8-15 NRSV)

In the first part of 1 Timothy 2, Paul expresses his desire for the knowledge of the truth to spread to all peoples (verses 3-7). But in what follows he implies that both men and women could be acting in such a way as to inhibit this. For each gender, he highlights two potential problems. Men may have issues with both anger and quarrelling (verse 8). Women may have issues with over-ostentatious adornment (verses 9-10) and failing to learn 'with quietness' (verses 11-12). It is this final issue which is our main concern here.

The first thing to notice about verses 11-12 is that they follow a very similar pattern to verses 9-10. This pattern can be seen in verses 9-10 by arranging them like this:

SENTENCE		⁹likewise also that women should adorn themselves in respectable apparel,	
ELABORATION		**with modesty**	**and self-control,**
BULLET	‹✗ not	with braided hair	and gold or pearls or costly attire, ✗›
BULLET	¹⁰but	with ‹✓ what is proper for women who profess godliness – with good works. ✓›[1]	

The annotation here is taken from the *Lexham High Definition New Testament*. Words in bold are highlighted by their position in the Greek text. The notation ‹✗ ...✗› indicates a *counterpoint* in the discourse. This is a negative point that is linked to, and adds emphasis to a positive point, indicted with ‹✓ ... ✓›. So the basic form of these verses is clear: there is a basic instruction (for women to be adorned with modesty and self-control), followed by a clarification. The clarification is in two parts. First there is a counterpoint ('not with...') and then a point ('but with...').

The form of verses 11-12 is very similar:

SENTENCE	¹¹Let a woman		
		learn **quietly**	with all submissiveness.
SENTENCE	¹²‹✗ • I do not **permit** a woman		
		to teach	or **to exercise authority over a man;** ✗›
ELABORATION	rather, ‹✓	**she is to remain quiet.** ✓›	

So, again, we have a basic instruction (for women to learn 'quietly'), followed by a clarification. This should not mean them 'teaching' or 'exercising authority' over a man, but does involve them remaining 'quiet'. The Greek word translated here as 'quietly' and 'quiet' suggests a 'state of quietness without disturbance' – certainly not necessarily

---

[1] Runge, S. E. (2008). *The Lexham High Definition New Testament: ESV Edition*. Logos Bible Software. Exported from Logos Bible Software 5, 11:57 01 May 2013.

implying absolute silence.² The Greek word translated as 'submissiveness' in verse 11 is a submissiveness in contrast to 'setting oneself up as controller'.³ In other words, Paul is concerned with women finding their right place in an ordered relationship structure. The Greek word translated 'to teach' is the word commonly used for teaching or instruction. Paul says overseers should be able to do it (1 Timothy 3:2), and instructs Timothy to do it (1 Timothy 4:11, 6:2). The word translated 'to exercise authority over' appears only here in the New Testament and its meaning is disputed.⁴ The precise meanings of 'to teach' and 'to exercise authority over' *in this particular context* we have yet to establish. However, one of the reasons for mapping out the structure of verses 11-12 as we have done above is to show that Paul is contrasting 'to teach' in verse 12 with 'learn quietly' in verse 11, and 'to exercise authority' in verse 12 with 'with all submissiveness [to the right order]' in verse 11. We shall come back to this observation later.

The form and syntax of the first clause in verse 12 is relatively unusual: *I do not permit a woman to x and/or to y*. However, we are given considerable help in understanding this verse through the very thorough scholarship of Andreas Köstenberger, who has considered every example of this kind of construction in both the biblical material and across virtually all the extant ancient Greek literature.⁵ Köstenberger concludes that we can divide these examples into two types. Remember, the construction presents two activities, x and y. The two possibilities he identifies are:

(a) x and y are both negative in themselves, and their combination is also negative

---

[2] In W. Bauer, F. W. Danker, W. F. Arndt, and F. W. Gingrich, *Greek-English Lexicon of the New Testament and Other Early Christian Literature* (Chicago: University of Chicago Press, 3rd edn, 1999), hereafter 'BDAG'.

[3] BDAG.

[4] BDAG suggests 'to assume a stance of independent authority, give orders to, dictate to'. Henry Scott Baldwin, 'An Important Word: *Authenteō* in 1 Timothy 2:12' in Köstenberger and Schreiner (eds.), *Women in the Church: An Analysis and Application of 1 Timothy 2:9-15* (2nd ed., Grand Rapids, Mich.: Baker, 2005), pp.39-51, suggests 'to control, to dominate,' 'to compel, to influence someone/something,' 'to assume authority over,' or 'to flout the authority of' as possibilities.

[5] Andreas J. Köstenberger, 'A Complex Sentence: the Syntax of 1 Timothy 2:12' in Köstenberger and Schreiner (eds.), *Women in the Church*, pp.53-84. The second edition is helpful for outlining the responses to Köstenberger's study since it was first published in 1995. His results seem to have stood the test of time.

(b) x and y are positive in themselves (or not necessarily negative), but in this context and in this combination they are negative.

For an example of the first type, consider Matthew 6:20:

> ... but store up for yourselves treasures in heaven, where neither moth nor rust consumes, and where thieves do not *break in* and [*oude*] *steal*.

Both *breaking in* and *stealing* are negative activities in themselves, and Jesus is presenting them here as negative in combination.

For an example of the second type, consider Acts 4:18:

> So they called them and charged them not *to speak* or [*mēde*] *teach* at all in the name of Jesus.

The rulers and elders of the people would not have considered speaking or teaching wrong in themselves. They are also not charging the apostles to be completely mute and not speak at all. But in the situation implied by the context (Peter and John speaking to the people and teaching them about Jesus' resurrection from the dead), they want to prohibit anything encompassed by 'speaking' or 'teaching' in relation to Jesus.

So we have two possibilities for translating 1 Timothy 2:12...

4.1.1. *Teaching and exercising authority in 1 Timothy 2:12 are both negative*

This suggests a translation like the following:

> Let a woman learn quietly with all submissiveness. I do not permit a woman to *teach falsely* or *aggressively domineer* a man, but she is to remain quiet.

Egalitarian readings of 1 Timothy tend to go down this line, because it leaves open the possibility that Paul might permit a woman to teach *true* doctrine to a man *without* trying to domineer him. That is, it allows the prohibition to be a special case that does not apply generally. We can picture what is implied by this interpretation of the verse like this:

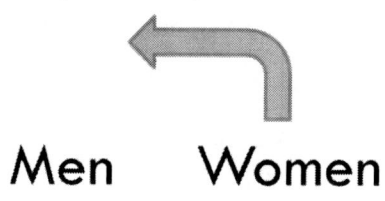

Men   Women

The claim is that Paul thinks teaching in authoritative leadership roles is equally accessible to men and women in principle. However, in this instance, certain women have abused the situation and are teaching untruths in a domineering way.

There are a number of variations on this view. For example, in a very influential book Richard and Catherine Kroeger suggest a very specific heresy in first century Ephesus as the background to Paul's teaching, involving Jewish-gnostic traditions combined with the Artemis cult. This elevated the status of women relative to men and perhaps suggested that the woman enlightened the man in the garden, even bestowing life upon him. Their suggested translation of verse 12 then goes like this:

> I do not permit a woman to teach nor to proclaim herself the author or originator of a man but she is to be in conformity [with the Scriptures][or that she keeps it a secret].[6]

Paul then refers back to Genesis 2 in verses 13 and 14 to show that in fact the man was made first, and to remind Timothy that (contrary to the claimed heresy) the woman was far from sinless. Moreover, verse 15, women need not deny their femininity by trying to take the male role.

The Kroegers' reconstruction of a 'proto-feminist' Ephesus where the Artemis cult affected the Ephesian churches in a very particular way has been comprehensively refuted by S.M. Baugh.[7] For example, those with authority at the temple of Artemis, including the priest of the temple and the sacred officers overseeing the cult were in fact all exclusively male. Nevertheless, the Kroegers' ideas have been surprisingly enduring. Take this recent paraphrase of verses 13 and 14 by Ian Paul:

> Don't believe the myths around you that women are superior to men. Eve sinned just as much as Adam did![8]

---

[6] Richard Kroeger and Catherine Kroeger, *I Suffer Not a Woman: Rethinking 1 Timothy 2:11-15 in Light of Ancient Evidence* (Grand Rapids, Mich.: Baker, 1992), p.103.
[7] S.M. Baugh, 'A Foreign World: Ephesus in the First Century', in in Köstenberger and Schreiner (eds.), *Women in the Church*, pp.13-38.
[8] Ian Paul, 'Women, Teaching and Authority', in Croft and Gooder (eds.), *Women and Men in Scripture and the Church*, p.38.

Michael Bird suggests the slightly more sober translation: *I do not permit a woman by <u>false</u> teaching to dominate a man.*[9] Rather than speculating about the Artemis cult, he then attempts to reconstruct the heresy some women may be teaching from the evidence of 1 Timothy alone. He concludes that certain women 'were trying to follow a pattern of life based on certain myths about Genesis'. He also claims their teaching 'probably tinkered with the story of Eve as well', although he offers no evidence for this apart from 2:13-15. This is the teaching Paul is prohibiting in 2:12 and refuting in 2:13-15.[10]

The suggestion of domineering behaviour in the negative-negative reading of 1 Timothy 2:12 does have some advantages. It links well to the context of some women behaving inappropriately in 1 Timothy 5. However, unlike chapter 5, the instruction here is framed more generally. Paul says, 'I do not permit' without any qualification or restriction.

The main disadvantage is that one has to supply 'teach *falsely*', which Paul could have made clear, as in 1:3 and 6:3. We have to speculate that Paul has in mind a *very particular* false teaching, which he then refutes in verses 13 and 14. It seems a very forced reading, given that Paul provides no indication in 2:12 that he is particularly concerned with the *content* of the teaching. On the contrary, the immediate context suggests that he is not concerned with content here. As we noted above, the simple structure contrasts teaching with 'learning' in verse 11. This strongly suggests he is concerned here with the *activity* of teaching, not so much its content.

Paul could have said: Let a woman <u>teach true doctrine</u> with all <u>humility</u>. I do not permit a woman to teach falsely or to aggressively domineer a man, but she is to remain <u>true/humble</u>. The egalitarian reading of verse 12 might then make more sense. But he did not.

4.1.2. *x and y are positive*

This suggests a translation such as:

Let a woman learn quietly with all submissiveness. I do not

---

[9] However, even this translation is somewhat wanting, supplying all sorts of connectives that are simply not there in the original text. In the original, 'to teach' and 'to exercise authority over' (translated here 'to dominate') are connected by [*oudé*] which simply means 'and not' or 'nor' or 'also not' or 'not even' (BDAG). It adds one negative statement to another.

[10] Michael Bird, *Bourgeois Babes,* section 'I Do Not Permit a Woman to Teach'...

permit a woman to teach or to exercise leadership authority over a man, but she is to remain quiet.

We can picture this way of interpreting the verses like this:

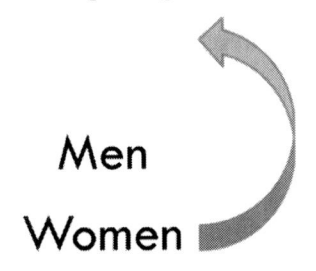

Men

Women ⟳

That is, Paul is assuming a complementarian relationship between men and women, based on his understanding of Genesis 2. Moreover, he is assuming that this applies not just in marriages but in church households, where roles of leadership authority should be restricted to men. What is happening in Ephesus is that certain women are reversing this order, just as Eve did in the garden. That is what he wishes to correct. Teaching can be a positive thing. Exercising leadership authority can be a positive thing. But in this combination and setting they are not appropriate.

The positive-positive reading of these verses has a number of advantages. It reads smoothly, without jumps or speculations, and fits well with surrounding material and context, including chapter 3 (as we shall see below). It certainly makes better sense of 2:13-14. Paul says 'For Adam was formed first, then Eve' to remind Timothy that it was the man, not the woman, who was given leadership responsibilities comparable to those of the first-born in ancient families and the responsibility to teach the woman the commands of Genesis 2:16-17. Paul says, 'and Adam was not deceived, but the woman was deceived and became a transgressor' to remind Timothy that when the woman in the garden assumed an inappropriate leadership role over the man, effectively teaching him to eat from the tree (Genesis 3:6), she was being *deceived*. It was a terrible thing, leading to transgression. It is this fundamental relational error that the women of Ephesus are in danger of repeating. Paul wishes them to avoid doing so.

However, even if we could agree that this is the smoothest and most obvious way to read 1 Timothy 2:11-14, many questions would remain. We would still have to work out *precisely* what kind of teaching

Paul has in mind. We have seen that the arguments are strongly against Paul merely prohibiting 'teaching which is domineering'. Likewise, any translation which suggests that 'teaching' and 'exercising authority' constitute together a single, unified idea (an 'hendiadys') in Paul's mind is probably unwarranted, given the separation of the terms in the original word order. On the other hand, it seems unlikely that they are entirely separate or separable. It is more likely that, while distinct, they are related in the situation Paul has in mind. If Paul were prohibiting women from teaching *full stop*, then this would contradict, for example, Titus 2:2-3, where older women are 'to teach what is good', thus training the younger women. Recall also that in Acts 18 we have at least one positive example of a woman teaching a man. Does 'to teach' in 2:12 encompass prophesy? Given 1 Corinthians 11:5, it cannot.

For more precise answers on the relation between 'to teach' and 'to exercise authority', we do have to look ahead to 1 Timothy 3.

4.2. 1 Timothy 3 and Titus 1 – a simple but neglected positive case for gender complementarity in church leadership roles

> ² Therefore an overseer must be above reproach, the husband of one wife, sober-minded, self-controlled, respectable, hospitable, able to teach, ³ not a drunkard, not violent but gentle, not quarrelsome, not a lover of money. ⁴ He must manage his own household well, with all dignity keeping his children submissive, ⁵ for if someone does not know how to manage his own household, how will he care for God's church? [...] ⁸ Deacons likewise must be dignified, not double-tongued, not addicted to much wine, not greedy for dishonest gain. [...] ¹¹ Their wives likewise must be dignified, not slanderers, but sober-minded, faithful in all things. (1 Timothy 3:2, 8, 11 ESV)

In 1 Timothy 2:12 Paul gives a prohibition concerning teaching and the exercise of authority. In 1 Timothy 3:1-13 he then gives some positive models of those who will exercise authority and teach. It seems extremely likely that these are related.

Moreover, gender is important in 1 Timothy 3:1-13. Overseers are very clearly *male* in Paul's description. Likewise in Titus 1, where overseers (Titus 1:7) are equivalent to elders (Titus 1:5). 'Deacons' in 1 Timothy 3:8-10, 12-13 are male, but this level of church leadership does seem to be more open to both genders. The NRSV of 1 Timothy 3:11 follows the Greek more closely in reading, 'Women likewise must be serious...' Paul might be referring to the wives of the deacons, or he might be thinking of female deacons – 'deaconesses'. Remember that he described Pheobe as a 'deacon' (Romans 16:1).

Notice also the strong connection Paul makes between managing a household and caring for the church (verses 4-5). Just as men lead and manage their households (verse 4), so men oversee, lead and care for the church (verse 5).

The models for elder and deacon and the different roles played by male and female in 1 Timothy 3:1-13 form part of the good order and pattern of behaviour by which the *household* of God may serve as a 'pillar and bulwark of the truth' (1 Timothy 3:15).

4.3. Putting it all together

So the answer to the question, 'What kind of teaching and authority does Paul have in mind in 1 Timothy 2:12?' is almost certainly, 'The kind of authority held by the overseer/elder of 1 Timothy 3:1-7 expressed in the kind of teaching through which he exercises that authority and leads the church household'.

That is, the context suggests that particular situation Paul has in mind is one where certain women in Ephesus are exercising (either implicitly or explicitly) leadership roles within church households, teaching the (gathered) church and exercising authority over men in the household of God in ways that should only be done by a *male* overseer. They are thus repeating the error of Eve in the very first household, subverting the created order of things and being deceived in doing so (1 Timothy 2:13-14). They should not be teaching the household as a whole; they should not be exercising authority over men in the household (1 Timothy 2:12). Instead of teaching the church, they should instead be learning, quietly and with full submission (1 Timothy 2:11), from a male overseer (chosen according to the criteria of 3:1-6).

5. Further Conclusions

I very much hope that it has been clear in this study that there is no disagreement between biblical complementarians and egalitarians on the fundamental equality of men and women before God. We affirm that the gospel declares the equal status of women in the justified community (Galatians 3:28), publically restoring their position as equal image-bearers of God (Genesis 1:27). Neither is there any dispute about the vital importance, value or worth of the gospel witness of women, or of the gospel ministry of women. Historians are agreed that in Greco-Roman culture, a culture in many ways hostile towards women, the Christian community provided a safe refuge, where women could enjoy equal status with men and grow in love and service. We are happy to agree with them, and greatly desire the same to be true today.

The present disagreement is about what this equality implies about access to leadership roles with the church. The modern egalitarian claim is that equality before God *must entail* equal access of men and women to *every* leadership role. This is where our understanding and submission to the Scriptures leads us to disagree.

As our discussion above on Jesus' teaching in Matthew 20:20-28 *et par* suggested, part of the issue here is how one understands the nature of Christian leadership. If one understood leadership to confer higher status or value on the leader relative to those being led, then restricting certain leadership roles to men might well then be in conflict with equality. But of course that is not the right way to understand leadership. The Christian understanding of leadership is that it involves assuming a *lower* status – that of a servant. So we do not find the restriction of certain leadership roles to men *automatically* in conflict with the equality of men and women before God. When Paul and Peter encourage husbands to exercise loving servant-hearted leadership within marriages, and wives to comply, this does not contradict their equality before God. When the roles of church-planting and the overlapping roles of oversight and eldership were taken by men in the early church, this likewise did not contradict the essential equality of men and women before God. When Timothy and Titus put into practice the instructions for appointing elders/overseers in 1 Timothy 3 and Titus 1, they would have understood clearly that they were to appoint men to those roles. But, again, this did not contradict the essential equality of men and women before God. In 1 Timothy 3, Paul was seeking to reform the churches of Ephesus in the form of godly households, under male leadership, within which men and women could work together to serve in the world as a 'pillar and bulwark of the truth'.

In the apostles' understanding, then, the gospel offered to women something other than merely an offer of equal opportunity in the contest for leadership roles. It was an invitation for women to join in constructive partnership with men in the promotion of the gospel in the world according to the ordered pattern of Genesis 2.

If complementarian convictions on this matter were the result of cultural conservatism or misogyny, then it would be right to rebuke us and call us to account. However, our claim remains that our position is supported by the clear teaching of the Scriptures, read carefully in both its historical and literary context, and according to the highest standards of scholarship. What is more, the complementarian claim remains that the asymmetric partnership between men and women in marriages and within church families, clearly attested in the Bible, is a beautiful one, *positively* contributing to the spread of gospel blessing and the glory of God in a broken world.

If you have enjoyed this book, you might like to consider

- *supporting the work of the Latimer Trust*
- *reading more of our publications*
- *recommending them to others*

See www.latimertrust.org for more information.

Latimer Publications

Latimer Studies

LS 01	The Evangelical Anglican Identity Problem	Jim Packer
LS 02	The ASB Rite A Communion: A Way Forward	Roger Beckwith
LS 03	The Doctrine of Justification in the Church of England	Robin Leaver
LS 04	Justification Today: The Roman Catholic and Anglican Debate	R. G. England
LS 05/06	Homosexuals in the Christian Fellowship	David Atkinson
LS 07	Nationhood: A Christian Perspective	O. R. Johnston
LS 08	Evangelical Anglican Identity: Problems and Prospects	Tom Wright
LS 09	Confessing the Faith in the Church of England Today	Roger Beckwith
LS 10	A Kind of Noah's Ark? The Anglican Commitment to Comprehensiveness	Jim Packer
LS 11	Sickness and Healing in the Church	Donald Allister
LS 12	Rome and Reformation Today: How Luther Speaks to the New Situation	James Atkinson
LS 13	Music as Preaching: Bach, Passions and Music in Worship	Robin Leaver
LS 14	Jesus Through Other Eyes: Christology in a Multi-faith Context	Christopher Lamb
LS 15	Church and State Under God	James Atkinson,
LS 16	Language and Liturgy	Gerald Bray, Steve Wilcockson, Robin Leaver
LS 17	Christianity and Judaism: New Understanding, New Relationship	James Atkinson
LS 18	Sacraments and Ministry in Ecumenical Perspective	Gerald Bray
LS 19	The Functions of a National Church	Max Warren
LS 20/21	The Thirty-Nine Articles: Their Place and Use Today	Jim Packer, Roger Beckwith
LS 22	How We Got Our Prayer Book	T.W. Drury, Roger Beckwith
LS 23/24	Creation or Evolution: a False Antithesis?	Mike Poole, Gordon Wenham
LS 25	Christianity and the Craft	Gerard Moate
LS 26	ARCIC II and Justification	Alister McGrath
LS 27	The Challenge of the Housechurches	Tony Higton, Gilbert Kirby
LS 28	Communion for Children? The Current Debate	A. A. Langdon
LS 29/30	Theological Politics	Nigel Biggar
LS 31	Eucharistic Consecration in the First Four Centuries and its Implications for Liturgical Reform	Nigel Scotland
LS 32	A Christian Theological Language	Gerald Bray
LS 33	Mission in Unity: The Bible and Missionary Structures	Duncan McMann
LS 34	Stewards of Creation: Environmentalism in the Light of Biblical Teaching	Lawrence Osborn
LS 35/36	Mission and Evangelism in Recent Thinking: 1974–1986	Robert Bashford
LS 37	Future Patterns of Episcopacy: Reflections in Retirement	Stuart Blanch
LS 38	Christian Character: Jeremy Taylor and Christian Ethics Today	David Scott
LS 39	Islam: Towards a Christian Assessment	Hugh Goddard
LS 40	Liberal Catholicism: Charles Gore and the Question of Authority	G. F. Grimes
LS 41/42	The Christian Message in a Multi-faith Society	Colin Chapman
LS 43	The Way of Holiness 1: Principles	D. A. Ousley

Latimer Publications

LS 44/45	The Lambeth Articles	V. C. Miller
LS 46	The Way of Holiness 2: Issues	D. A. Ousley
LS 47	Building Multi-Racial Churches	John Root
LS 48	Episcopal Oversight: A Case for Reform	David Holloway
LS 49	Euthanasia: A Christian Evaluation	Henk Jochemsen
LS 50/51	The Rough Places Plain: AEA 1995	
LS 52	A Critique of Spirituality	John Pearce
LS 53/54	The Toronto Blessing	Martyn Percy
LS 55	The Theology of Rowan Williams	Garry Williams
LS 56/57	Reforming Forwards? The Process of Reception and the Consecration of Woman as Bishops	Peter Toon
LS 58	The Oath of Canonical Obedience	Gerald Bray
LS 59	The Parish System: The Same Yesterday, Today And For Ever?	Mark Burkill
LS 60	'I Absolve You': Private Confession and the Church of England	Andrew Atherstone
LS 61	The Water and the Wine: A Contribution to the Debate on Children and Holy Communion	Roger Beckwith, Andrew Daunton-Fear
LS 62	Must God Punish Sin?	Ben Cooper
LS 63	Too Big For Words? The Transcendence of God and Finite Human Speech	Mark D. Thompson
LS 64	A Step Too Far: An Evangelical Critique of Christian Mysticism	Marian Raikes
LS 65	The New Testament and Slavery: Approaches and Implications	Mark Meynell
LS 66	The Tragedy of 1662: The Ejection and Persecution of the Puritans	Lee Gatiss
LS 67	Heresy, Schism & Apostasy	Gerald Bray
LS 68	Paul in 3D: Preaching Paul as Pastor, Story-teller and Sage	Ben Cooper
LS69	Christianity and the Tolerance of Liberalism: J.Gresham Machen and the Presbyterian Controversy of 1922-1937	Lee Gatiss
LS70	An Anglican Evangelical Identity Crisis: The Churchman–Anvil Affair of 1981-4	Andrew Atherstone
LS71	Empty and Evil: The worship of other faiths in 1 Corinthians 8-10 and today	Rohintan Mody
LS72	To Plough or to Preach: Mission Strategies in New Zealand during the 1820s	Malcolm Falloon
LS73	Plastic People: How Queer Theory is changing us	Peter Sanlon
LS74	Deification and Union with Christ: Salvation in Orthodox and Reformed thought	Slavko Eždenci
LS75	As It Is Written: Interpreting the Bible with Boldness	Benjamin Sargent
LS76	Light From Dark Ages? An Evangelical Critique of Celtic Spirituality	Marian Raikes
LS77	The Ethics of Usury	Ben Cooper
LS78	For Us and For Our Salvation: 'Limited Atonement' in the Bible, Doctrine, History and Ministry	Lee Gatiss
LS79	Positive Complementarianism: The Key Biblical Texts	Ben Cooper

Latimer Publications

Latimer Briefings

LB01	The Church of England: What it is, and what it stands for	R. T. Beckwith
LB02	Praying with Understanding: Explanations of Words and Passages in the Book of Common Prayer	R. T. Beckwith
LB03	The Failure of the Church of England? The Church, the Nation and the Anglican Communion	A. Pollard
LB04	Towards a Heritage Renewed	H.R.M. Craig
LB05	Christ's Gospel to the Nations: The Heart & Mind of Evangelicalism Past, Present & Future	Peter Jensen
LB06	Passion for the Gospel: Hugh Latimer (1485–1555) Then and Now. A commemorative lecture to mark the 450th anniversary of his martyrdom in Oxford	A. McGrath
LB07	Truth and Unity in Christian Fellowship	Michael Nazir-Ali
LB08	Unworthy Ministers: Donatism and Discipline Today	Mark Burkill
LB09	Witnessing to Western Muslims: A Worldview Approach to Sharing Faith	Richard Shumack
LB10	Scarf or Stole at Ordination? A Plea for the Evangelical Conscience	Andrew Atherstone
LB11	How to Write a Theology Essay	Michael P. Jensen
LB12	Preaching: A Guidebook for Beginners	Allan Chapple
LB13	Justification by Faith: Orientating the Church's teaching and practice to Christ (Toon Lecture 1)	Michael Nazir-Ali
LB14	"Remember Your Leaders": Principles and Priorities for Leaders from Hebrews 13	Wallace Benn
LB15	How the Anglican Communion came to be and where it is going	Michael Nazir-Ali

Latimer Books

GGC	God, Gays and the Church: Human Sexuality and Experience in Christian Thinking	eds. Lisa Nolland, Chris Sugden, Sarah Finch
WTL	The Way, the Truth and the Life: Theological Resources for a Pilgrimage to a Global Anglican Future	eds. Vinay Samuel, Chris Sugden, Sarah Finch
AEID	Anglican Evangelical Identity – Yesterday and Today	J.I.Packer, N.T.Wright
IB	The Anglican Evangelical Doctrine of Infant Baptism	John Stott, Alec Motyer
BF	Being Faithful: The Shape of Historic Anglicanism Today	Theological Resource Group of GAFCON
TPG	The True Profession of the Gospel: Augustus Toplady and Reclaiming our Reformed Foundations	Lee Gatiss
SG	Shadow Gospel: Rowan Williams and the Anglican Communion Crisis	Charles Raven
TTB	Translating the Bible: From Willliam Tyndale to King James	Gerald Bray
PWS	Pilgrims, Warriors, and Servants: Puritan Wisdom for Today's Church	ed. Lee Gatiss
PPA	Preachers, Pastors, and Ambassadors: Puritan Wisdom for Today's Church	ed. Lee Gatiss
CWP	The Church, Women Bishops and Provision: The Integrity of Orthodox Objections to the Proposed Legislation Allowing Women Bishops	
TSF	The Truth Shall Set You Free: Global Anglicans in the 21st Century	ed. Charles Raven

Latimer Publications

ANGLICAN FOUNDATIONS SERIES

FWC	The Faith We Confess: An Exposition of the 39 Articles	Gerald Bray
AF02	The 'Very Pure Word of God': The Book of Common Prayer as a Model of Biblical Liturgy	Peter Adam
AF03	Dearly Beloved: Building God's People Through Morning and Evening Prayer	Mark Burkill
AF04	Day by Day: The Rhythm of the Bible in the Book of Common Prayer	Benjamin Sargent
AF05	The Supper: Cranmer and Communion	Nigel Scotland

Lightning Source UK Ltd.
Milton Keynes UK
UKOW02f0332061016

284566UK00001B/12/P

9 781906 327217